Born Again, Now What?

D1640769

There is Always Faith!

Born Again, Now What?

Ten Basic Things To Do After Salvation

Noreen N. Henry

Foreword by Nadine Fortune BSN RN

Trilogy Christian Publishers A Wholly Owned Subsidiary of Trinity Broadcasting Network 2442 Michelle Drive Tustin, CA 92780

Rights Department, 2442 Michelle Drive, Tustin, CA 92780.

Trilogy Christian Publishing/ TBN and colophon are trademarks of Trinity Broadcasting Network.

For information about special discounts for bulk purchases, please contact Trilogy Christian Publishing.

Trilogy Disclaimer: The views and content expressed in this book are those of the author and may not necessarily reflect the views and doctrine of Trilogy Christian Publishing or the Trinity Broadcasting Network.

Manufactured in the United States of America

10 9 8 7 6 5 4 3 2 1

Library of Congress Cataloging-in-Publication Data is available.

B-ISBN#: 978-1-68556-330-1

E-ISBN#: 978-1-68556-331-8

Preface

The purpose of this book is to explain that there are things we need to begin doing (individually) as soon as we are born again (born again spiritually that is). We are now born of the Spirit and have a new life; this is why we set our sights on heavenly things by doing things differently.

After we have accepted our Lord and Savior, there are things we need to learn to do. As I often say, "unlearn and relearn." We are to not look at things from the world's perspective anymore, instead, we are to look at things from a heavenly perspective (see Rom. 12:2) that is the unseen realm.

This book will enlighten and open the eyes of your understanding to receive the revelation that we have things to do when we are born again. It will explain about ten basic things to start doing right away. It's not just being born again, there's much more to it. You will need take heed to the revelation of the things to do now that you're saved.

Born again, spiritually, now what?

When I learned about being born again, I didn't know that it meant spiritually. Many years ago, I didn't know what born again was, let alone that we have things we must do. I didn't know that we are spirit beings placed in a body. With learning the things of God, it makes sense to me now to know that it is my spirit that is born again. This is a subject that needs to be properly explained so people can fully understand it because there is a lot of error being taught, or not taught at all.

Before being born again, I handled life through my own eyes, from my parents and family, and even from the media, television, radio, etc. But now that I am born again spiritually, I handle my life from God's perspective. This is why we are to learn about the spiritual things because, for me, I was living by earthly things and even though the earth belongs to the Lord, it is the devil's playground for our lives. I know this to be true because my life changed for the better when I started learning and applying the ten basic things listed in this book.

Join me as we learn what to do now that we are born again, spiritually, that is.

Foreword

Born Again, Now What? provides much needed guidance on how to pray, worship and develop a relationship with our Heavenly Father.

I was born again after being in a religious cult for over twenty years. The religious cult I was raised in was void of the love of our Heavenly Father and Jesus Christ. I whole heartedly believed I was serving God in truth and righteousness. The cult threatened excommunication if the members failed to follow the many legalistic rules of the leaders. I often felt guilt when I participated in the shunning of an excommunicated cult member. I served as a Registered Nurse for ten of the years that I was a member of the cult. I felt such freedom while working with patients. I always placed myself in the mindset that I would treat each patient as if I were caring for a family member. As a nurse I begin each shift by reading my patients extensive medical and social history. I knew all their business before I even met them! It felt so good to treat my vulnerable patients with love despite the fact that I just read about their many "sins" at the beginning of the shift. I now know that I was extending unconditional love to my patients. The same love our Heavenly Father extends to all when they accept his invitation and are spiritually born again.

God used many believers over many years, including Coach Noreen, to tell me the good news. I was given my first Bible in my twenties by a co-worder. Another co-worker invited me to a Women's Retreat at her church. witnessed unconditional love and couldn't get enough of it! I accepted Christ as my savior and left the cult. I was free! I was promptly excommunicated by the cult and my lifelong friends were forbidden to talk to me. My co-workers covered me with prayer during this difficult time. I knew there was no going back.

Before being born again, I followed the manmade rules of the cult. I did not know how to move forward in my new spiritual life. Coach Noreen's book *Born Again, Now What?* reads like conversations with a wise, yet patient friend. I am so glad you were led to her teachings! Coach Noreen clearly presents ten steps to guide believers during all stages of their spiritual journey. God loves new beginnings!

Nadine Fortune BSN RN
Transformational Coach
www.FortunateLiving.org

Endorsements for "Born Again, Now What"

It is with great honor that I write this endorsement for my sister in Christ. Noreen and I met what feels like a lifetime ago the bond was immediate. Noreen's passion and purpose are impactful and transferring to those she leads and coaches. I see her heart for God, her passion, and her gift for leading others to Christ and helping them to get and remain unstuck. I witnessed her embrace, empower, educate, and equip others to identify, and align with their God given purpose to live peaceful and fulfilling lives. And incorporating these ten basic things to do when born again puts you in the path to living victoriously God's way.

Marissa L. Bloedoorn, M.Sc., DTM
CEO TCS Consulting LLC
CEO & Editor in Chief, "OWN It!"
Magazine & Publishing LLC

This book for the newly born-again Christian provides encouragement, gives a sense of understanding on how to use these tools such as learning how to pray, how to fast, and mostly develop a closer relationship with God our father. This book inspired me as a Christian for many years to use these passages as a reminder of God's abiding love and how to strengthen my walk with God. This book is a great valuable tool to guide newer Christians.

Evangelist Michelle Davenport MSN, PHN, FCN, RN
Doctorate of Nursing Practice
sistermcb@msn.com

Born Again, Now What? Being "born again" is like a newborn baby brought home from the hospital: helpless and totally dependent on the loving care, attention, nurturing, and rearing provided by its parents. Likewise, are you as a born-again Believer. In her book, *Born Again, Now What?* my dear friend, Noreen Henry, shares from her heart reflections of what she would have ministered to herself in her early years as a new disciple of Christ. This book reminds me of an old adage: "When a tree grows crooked, it cannot be made straight again". As you invite Holy Spirit [your divine Teacher] to guide you through this biblically fortified tool, you will be well on your way to growing up straight and deeply rooted as a new Believer and disciplined follower of Jesus Christ.

Yvette S. Ellington
Associate Pastor
Victorious Living Fellowship, Inc.

To have a complete understanding of something there are 3 elements that must be addressed: the WHAT, the WHY, and the HOW. When the "WHAT" is missing, there is a lack of clarity. When the "WHY" is missing there is a lack of significance or motivation. When the "How" is missing, there is lack of action and direction.

In this book, *Born Again, Now What?*, Noreen N. Henry masterfully provides insight into all 3 elements. What is Salvation? Why is it significant? What do I do now?

To know Noreen N. Henry is to understand that Victorious Living is her lived perspective rooted in the Word of God. It is not an erroneous conjecture, but rather the results of a true grasp of what Salvation is.

I invite you to read, reflect, and revisit this book often as you grow in wisdom and understanding.

Dr. JoWanda Rollins-Fells
Spirit of Excellence LLC
www.drrealtalk.com

Noreen has done a wonderful job of carrying out the Great Commission through this work. It is one thing to desire a better life, it is another level to truly understand what salvation means and what it looks like in a tangible way to walk in it. The way that this book is laid out is in such a way that you can easily understand and walk through the steps. What I am most moved and inspired by is gaining the understanding that it is not just about believing in Jesus but having an everyday walk that shows that belief. It is so important that we don't get overwhelmed by religion but rather build a true relationship with our Savior. Noreen's way of tackling these topics such as prayer, studying the Bible and Fasting will help anyone looking to go deeper in their walk. If you are looking to take a deeper dive in what it looks like practically to be born again and what the Bible says to show us how to live out this walk, this book is a great place to start.

Erica Latrice
Empowerment Speaker, Author & TV Host
www.EricaLatrice.com

Noreen Henry has developed and launched a number of book projects. They have all been impactful and transformational. This book project is no different. I am always looking for ways to go deeper mentally, emotionally, and especially spiritually. This book helped me to a deep dive with my spiritual connection with God and was so healing. It is really great to read but having activities to help you throughout is PHENOM-ENAL!! It allows you to take in information mentally and take action and do the necessary work. This is so vital to being able to learn and transform. Noreen is a phenomenal coach and spiritual leader. This book is a necessity. Get your copy now and work with Noreen 1:1, it will be life changing.

Chanel Spencer
Founder & CEO
www.maxevol.com

Acknowledgments

Thank You my heavenly Father, for who You are and all You do. Thank You, Lord, for showing me that there are things we must do with our salvation. Last, but not least, thank you Holy Spirit for leading and guiding me in this. Thank You Lord for opening my spiritual eyes and giving me the revelation to write this book, *Born Again, Now What: 10 Basic Things to Do After Salvation*.

I thank those that continually pray for me and support me. Without your prayers and support, I would not be where I am today, and the only thing I covet is prayers.

Thank you for the pastors and ministries that I have learned from over the years. This helped to shape me spiritually. Thank you for doing as the Lord led you, for that has helped me grow in the Lord tremendously.

Dedication

I dedicate *Born Again Now What? 10 Things to Do After Salvation*, to my family, friends, associates, who are the love of my life. My wish is that they learn what has to be done with salvation to have the victorious life we are meant to have, and in turn, help build up God's kingdom. I also wish for all to be saved, like the Lord, I don't want anyone to perish (2 Peter 3:9).

I also dedicate this to myself. Because of continuing to live my life, practically the same, after being saved then learning years later that there is so much more to salvation, this book would not have been possible.

"Salvation"

Are you saved? Do you know what it means to be saved?

Salvation means preservation from trouble or danger, or to protect or spare, etc. Salvation is deliverance from sin and its consequences; Salvation is God's gift through Christ, to save men's souls. Save men's souls from what? Saves us from eternal damnation, saves us from hell.

After all is said and done, where do you want to spend eternity, hell or heaven? Please note that where you spend eternity is your choice; it's *your* choice...

Please make the right choice by choosing heaven for your *own* sake by choosing God; because, when we pass on from earth, our spirit lives on forever, and like Jesus, I want everyone to be in heaven.

If you are not saved and would like to be (which is highly suggested), please say the following prayer to ensure that your eternal home will be in heaven with our heavenly Father and that you'll live an abundant life while on earth.

SALVATION PRAYER:

Dear Lord,

I acknowledge that I have been a sinner and that I need Your salvation. You said in Your Word that if I confess with my mouth the Lord Jesus Christ and believe in my heart that Jesus was born of a virgin mother, God raised Him from the dead and, He is now seated at the right hand of the Father that I will be saved. I am inviting you now to come into my heart. I believe that you died for me, and I believe that you rose again from the dead, and that you are now seated at the right hand of God. Thank you for your blood and thank you for dying for me. I receive you now as my Lord and personal Savior, in Jesus's name. Thank you for forgiving me for all my sins. Thank You for making me Your child. Help me learn to follow Your will and Your way for the rest of my life. In Jesus's name I pray, amen.

Name   Date

You are now saved; your name is written in the Lamb's book of life. Angels are rejoicing in heaven that you are saved, hallelujah!

Scriptures:

That if you confess with your mouth the Lord Jesus and believe in your heart that God has raised Him from the dead, you will be saved. For with the heart one believes unto righteousness, and with the mouth confession is made unto salvation.

Romans 10:9–10

"Therefore, if anyone *is* in Christ, *he is* a new creation; old things have passed away; behold, all things have become new" (2 Cor. 5:17).

Please contact me for the next step in your walk with the Lord.

Via email: victoriouslivingministries7@gmail.com

In writing: 1803 Neried Avenue, #143, Bronx, NY 10466

In the meantime, you'll need to find a Bible-based, gospel and faith-based church home to get taught the unadulterated Word of God, and to have fellowship with other believers. (I encourage you to ask God to show you where to go.)

Understand that there is much more to salvation once you are born again.

I pray, Lord, that each individual reader opens their heart to agree with what Your Word gives us to do after being born again spiritually. That they take heed to the promises that You give in Your Word as we properly apply Your words to our lives. Thank You, Father God, for the massive opening of great revelation that You are pouring out, in Your name, Lord. It is so.

Table of Contents

Introduction

Salvation is quite a broad topic, and many people don't realize how broad of a topic it is.

Paraphrasing from yourdictionary.com, the definition of salvation is the saving of human beings from sin and its consequences, which include death and separation from God. Salvation is the saving of a person from sin or evil. To be saved from danger or difficulty.

There was a time in my life that I didn't know that there is much more to salvation. I was born again (spiritually) for many years before I got the revelation that salvation entails a lot more than just being saved and just going to church. When you are born again, you have to change from the inside out and live from a spiritual perspective.

Formerly, I lived my life on my terms before learning about salvation, and when I got saved, learning many years later that there is much more to just being saved. Also because of living life on my terms instead of my heavenly Father's terms, things in my life weren't getting any better until I began doing these ten things.

When I was born again, spiritually, I attended church, read my Bible, prayed a little, changed a little. The pastor at the church I attended told me to come to church as much as I can. That's it. I should have been taught I have to:

- Change my ways to God's ways.

- That I have to do more than go to church.

- That I need to learn the things of God and apply it to my life.

- That I have to change my mindset.

- That I have promises from God, favor, healing, so many things.

When I was attending Sunday school in my early teen years, the Sunday school teacher had us memorize scripture each week. I don't remember the scripture verses we were memorizing, and again, we weren't taught that we were to apply the scripture to our lives. Even though we weren't getting proper teaching, I loved Sunday school.

A lot of the basic things to do when we are saved is what is missing and that is why many are born again but their lives haven't changed for the better. As I've changed my life by properly applying the Word of

God to it, I've been told things like, I'm weird, I'm living in a fantasy world, etc. If people knew how to properly apply the Word of God to their lives, it would be understood that I am on the right track, and I wouldn't be called those things.

Salvation involves a lot more than being saved (spiritually), and there are things we must do after we are saved (spiritually) to live the life we're supposed to be living as stated in John 10:10b.

For me, this is the missing element in churches/ministries. We need to know what to do after we are saved; we don't just go to church every week because there are basic things we have to doing, and we also have a role to play because we are here for a purpose.

This book will explain the basic things we have to do now that we are saved (born again spiritually). It will help people to have a life full of victories, peace, abundance, knowledge, wisdom, and many more things. One of my sayings is "we have so much in God, we just have to learn it." And not just learn it, but properly apply God's Word to our lives.

It is often said that life with God is an adventure. I've added that, it is also the same with Satan, life is an adventure. It's about who we want the adventure with.

I want my life to be adventurous with God because life works best with God in it, and in the end, we win.

With salvation, we'll have a great adventure with the Lord once we know what we need to do with our salvation.

It is vitally important that we learn what we are to do now that we are saved spiritually because our lives, literally, depend on it.

Let's begin.

Prayer:

Heavenly Father,

I come to You Lord as You say to come boldly to Your throne of grace. I pray on behalf of the saved and the to-be saved that You Lord, open their spiritual eyes of understanding and ears to hear what the Spirit of the Lord is saying and to take heed to Your will and Your way Lord. I pray Lord that each individual reader understands that we have basic things to do now that we are saved spiritually, will take heed to Your Word, and follow the plan of God for their lives. In the name of the Lord, it is done.

Let's begin our journey of born again, now what?

1: Study the Word of God (The Bible) and Apply it to Your Life

The very first thing we are to do when we are born again is to seek God first, see Matthew 6:33 and Luke 12:31. In order to seek God first, we have to learn about Him in the Bible. So, the first thing in our journey after being born again spiritually is to study the Bible. [Note: The Bible is spiritual law.]

Reading and studying the Bible is spiritual food for us. As being born again is spiritual, as we learn of God through the Bible, we get nourished and grow in our spiritual life.

<u>The Bible means</u>:

B – Basic

I – Instructions

B – Before

L – Leaving

E – Earth

These meanings are true because as I've studied the Bible and properly applied it to my life, things are so much better. Life is easier to handle.

Everything in life has instructions. As simple as it is to bake a cake, there are instructions to follow. If the instructions to bake a cake are not followed, the cake won't taste good. There are instructions on how to be skilled to work in a profession. There are instructions on how to drive a car. Everything has instructions, and we have our life instructions in the Word of God, the Bible.

ಬೊ ಞ ಬೊ ಞ ಬೊ ಞ ಬೊ ಞ ಬೊ ಞ ಬೊ ಞ ಬೊ ಞ ಬೊ ಞ ಬೊ ಞ

Joshua 1:8 says:

This Book of the Law shall not depart out of

your mouth, but you shall meditate on it day and night, that you may observe and do according to all that is written in it. For then you shall make your way prosperous, and then you shall deal wisely and have good success.

Depart: leave, especially in order to start a journey. To deviate from (an accepted, prescribed, or traditional course of action).

Meditate: think deeply or carefully about (something).

Observe: notice or perceive (something) and register it as being significant.

Prosperous: successful in material terms; flourishing financially. Bringing wealth and success.

Wisely: in a way that shows experience, knowledge, and good judgment.

Success: the accomplishment of an aim or purpose.

We are not to depart or deviate from the book of the law (meaning the Bible), but we have to meditate on it by thinking deeply or focusing our minds for a period of time day and night that we can observe, notice, or perceive and register as being significant and do accordingly, as is stated, to all that is written in it for us to do or not do. For then we shall make our way prosperous, successful, flourishing, bringing wealth and success, and then we shall deal wisely, having or showing experience, knowledge, and good judgment, and have good success, accomplishment of an aim or purpose.

The book of the law is the Bible. In order to study the Bible, you'll have to purchase a Bible and purchase Bible helps. Bible helps are: a concordance, a Bible dictionary, various versions of the Bible (among them make sure to have study Bibles) a Bible commentary, etc. Using all these tools will help you to understand and breakdown the scriptures in the Bible in order to properly apply the Bible to your life because that is the goal of studying it, doing what it says.

My book, *Are You in God's Will: Do You Know That You Have to Choose?* talks about doing what the Bible says. When we do what the Word of God says, it makes for a better life all around. We gain so much more in life in a positive way.

Some Bible translations are:

King James Version, which is the originally translated version from The Geneva Bible.

NASB: word-for-word translation.

Amplified: which is an English language translation

New Living Translation: which is a life application Bible.

The Message: which is a reading Bible, not a study Bible as it's more like a novel

To study the Bible, we are to read the scripture, look up the meaning of key words, and read the scripture with the meaning of the words to make it more understandable. Then once we study and meditate on the Word, we apply it to our lives. For example, the Bible says in Exodus 20:15, to not steal. In applying the Bible to our lives, we will remember this scripture and not steal.

While studying the Bible, we are to ask ourselves the following questions:

*Who?

*What?

*Where?

*How?

*Why?

We ask these questions as we are studying the Bible to understand the time and season of what was going on at that time and to know how to properly apply the Bible to our lives.

For example, throughout the Bible, it talks about women not wearing makeup on their faces or wearing jewelry. One reason for this was idolizing. We are not idolizing things because it will make our focus wrong. We are to always put God first. So, technically this scripture only applies if you are idolizing makeup and jewelry. For me, I don't see anything wrong with make-up and jewelry as long as it doesn't interfere with your relationship with the Lord.

Another example, the Bible says in Galatians 5:22–23, NIV, *"But the fruit of the Spirit is love, joy, peace, for-bearance, kindness, goodness, faithfulness, gentleness and self-control. Against such things there is no law."* The fruit of the spirit is love, joy, peace, patience, goodness, kind-ness, and self-control. These are key words to look up to see the true meaning of the words. This helps to properly apply the Word to our lives.

Being born again is a spiritual thing. This is learning things from a spiritual standpoint, and it's all internal changes. As the internal is changed, the external will be changed. It's a work from the inside out.

These are examples of properly and rightly divid-ing the Word of God to understand the principles and how to apply them to our lives. It is important to apply the Word of God to our lives because it is our guidebook to use when we are born again spiritually. As we go by God's guidebook, it is a preventative from hurt, making the wrong choices, etc. As we apply God's Word to our lives, we will be better ourselves and we will treat others better too. So much good stuff.

I'll give you one more example. Philippians 4:8 says meditate on these things:

Finally, brethren, whatever things are true, whatever things are noble, whatever things are just, whatever things are pure, whatever things are lovely, whatever things are of good report, if there is any virtue and if there is anything praiseworthy—meditate on these things.

When we think on what is true, noble, etc., we will always think good things. *This is what God wants us to do.* It makes for a better life all around. No matter how someone behaves, when we think on Philippians 4:8, we will see the good in them instead of the bad behavior.

With using Philippians 4:8, if my thoughts start to become negative, I think about, if it is true, if it is of a good report, is there any virtue, etc., and if not, then I change my thoughts. [Note: we have the power to change our thoughts. I'll talk about that in another book.]

This is what we are to do with our salvation.

An example of breaking down the scriptures:

The Word (the Bible) says to study to show thyself approved.

Study *and* be eager *and* do your utmost to present yourself to God approved (tested by trial), a workman who has no cause to be ashamed, correctly analyzing *and* accurately dividing [rightly handling and skillfully teaching] the Word of Truth.

2 Timothy 2:15 (AMPC)

Study: the devotion of time and attention to acquiring knowledge on an academic subject, especially by means of books

Approved: officially agree to or accept as satisfactory

Present: to act the part of

Correctly: in a way that is true, factual, or appropriate; accurately

Analyzing: examine methodically and in detail the constitution or structure of (something, especially information), typically for purposes of explanation and interpretation

Accurately: in a way that is correct in all details; exactly

Dividing: separate or be separated into parts

Rightly: correctly

Handling: manage

Truth: the quality or state of being true.

I can testify to the fact that life works so much better when we do things God's way. One of my quotes is "we have so much in life with God, we just have to learn it."

The Bible basically teaches us how to live life here on earth. As we do what the Bible says, the following will occur:

- We make choices that will make for a good life.

- We will treat others well no matter how they treat us.

- We will love unconditionally.

- We will know who to have in our inner circle.

- We will learn to see the truth in people to know if they are good for us or not.

- We will have peace, stay in joy, and happiness no matter what

- We will live a great life, the life of our dreams.

- We will always have help from the Lord.

The Bible is a guide that protects us from hurt and harm as we do as is said. For example, the Bible says not to commit adultery, meaning to only be with the person you married until death do you part. In this way, both parties stay together and don't think about being with someone else. On the other hand, when people commit adultery, all those involved gets hurt, especially the children.

It is so important to study the Bible and properly apply it to your life. It is our guidebook for living a great life on earth. It also promises in Luke 12:28, "...blessed are those who hear the Word of God and keep it."

Questions/Things to Think About

1. What is the first thing we should do when we are born again?

_____

_____

_____

_____

_____

_____

2. What is the purpose of the Bible?

_____

_____

_____

_____

_____

_____

3. How does the Bible help you in your life circumstances?

_____

_____

_____

_____

_____

_____

_____

4. How do you properly apply the Bible to your life?

_____

_____

_____

_____

_____

_____

5. What does Joshua 1:8 say we must do?

_____

_____

_____

_____

_____

_____

_____

6. Why is the Bible important?

_____

_____

_____

_____

_____

_____

7. Why is it important to study the Bible?

_____

_____

_____

_____

_____

_____

8. What questions do we ask ourselves as we study the Bible?

_____

_____

_____

_____

_____

9. As we study the Bible, what are two things that
    occur?

    _____

    _____

    _____

    _____

    _____

    _____

10. What does the Bible help to prevent as we ap-
    ply it to our lives?

    _____

    _____

    _____

    _____

    _____

    _____

2: Learn Who We Are in Our Heavenly Father and Have a Relationship with Him

Another important "must do" after we are born again spiritually, is to learn who we are in the Lord and develop a relationship with Him.

We start by doing as is said in Matthew 6:33, *"But seek first the kingdom of God and His righteousness and all these things shall be added to you."* Submit your life to His Lordship, follow His commands given in His Word. Be obedient to His Word. Make your relationship with God the number one priority.

When we know who we are in Him, we are bold, confident, and courageous, we don't put up with the nonsense from the enemy anymore. We live from a place of power (2 Tim. 1:7) and authority (Matt. 28:18). We live in perfect peace, the peace that surpasses all understanding (Phil. 4:7). We gain so much when we know who we are and have a relationship with our Lord and Savior.

Ephesians 1:2–6, KJV, explains who we are in Christ (our Messiah).

> *Grace be to you, and peace, from God our Father, and from the Lord Jesus Christ. Blessed be the God and Father of our Lord Jesus Christ, who hath blessed us with all spiritual blessings in heavenly places in Christ: According as he hath chosen us in him before the foundation of the world, that we should be holy and without blame before him in love: Having predestinated us unto the adoption of children by Jesus Christ to himself, according to the good pleasure of his will, To the praise of the glory of his grace, wherein he hath made us accepted in the beloved.*

How to you develop a relationship with the Lord?

By studying His Word (the Bible) and applying it to your life through prayer and just speaking with

Him. We don't see God, but He is in our hearts. My relationship with Him guides me in the right direction. When I listen to the voice of God, I know that I'm doing the right thing, and I will have success, as it is said in Joshua 1:8.

Here are six things you can do to develop your relationship with God:

1. **Take the time to touch bases with God**, always acknowledging and giving thanks for His presence.

2. **Invite Him to come close**, to sit with you at your heart's kitchen table and just hang out.

3. **Just talk to the Lord.** Some days this will feel like pouring out your heart. Other days, it will be casual chit-chat. Occasionally, all you'll be able to manage is, "Here I am, Lord. Please be with me."

4. **Listen to Him.** Remember to make it a two-way conversation and expect to hear from God, just as you would from a trusted friend. God wants you to know how much He loves you. He wants to offer support and guidance to you. If you don't take the time to listen, you won't hear His "voice." For me, this communication from

God comes in any of various forms: thoughts, feelings, music, reading, nature, other people, or circumstances.

5. **Make contact throughout your day.** Being in touch with God doesn't have to be only during times of meditation or prayer. It can be while you're on the run, when you're in the midst of activities, or when you have a moment's break. I constantly make contact with the Lord, all day long.

6. **Take action, right away, when you hear God's voice.** If you feel God is guiding you or telling you something, take action on it as soon as possible. The insight you receive may only show you where to take the next step, but once you've taken that step, the following step will appear in front of you.

I know this is a lot that you are learning, but don't worry about the time with developing a relationship, just develop it, as it does get better and better in time. I was saved a long time before I developed a proper relationship with the Lord, thus the reason for this book.

When we learn who we are in Him:

*We will know that regardless of what happens, we are blameless and free of accusation (Col. 1:22).

*We will know that we are a child of God (John 1:2).

*We will learn who we are in Him, we will know that we are part of the true vine, a channel of our Lord's life (John 15:1,5).

*We will know that we are sons of God: God is spiritually our Father (Rom. 8:14, 15).

*We will know that we are more than conquerors through Christ who loves us (Rom. 8:37).

*We will know we have been placed into Christ by God's doing (1 Cor. 1:30).

*We will know that we are united to the Lord and are one spirit with Him (1 Cor. 6:17).

*We will know we are being changed into the likeness of Christ (2 Cor. 3:18).

*We will know we are a new creation (2 Cor. 5:17).

*We will know we have been made righteous (2 Cor. 5:21).

*We will know that we are given strength in exchange for weakness (2 Cor. 12:10).

*We will know that we have been crucified with Christ and it is no longer I who live, but Christ lives in me.

The life we are now living is Christ's life (Gal. 2:20).

*We will know that we were chosen in Christ before the foundation of the world to be holy and without blame before Him (Eph. 1:4).

*We will know that we have been made alive together with Christ (Eph. 2:5).

*We will know that we are God's workmanship...His handiwork...born anew in Him to do His work (Eph. 2:10).

*We will know that we have direct access to God through the Spirit (Eph. 2:18).

*We will know that we have been rescued from the domain of Satan's rule and transferred to the kingdom of Christ (Col. 1:13).

*We will know we have been redeemed and forgiven of all our sins. The debt against us has been cancelled (Col. 1:14).

*We will know that the Lord Himself is in us (Col. 1:27).

*We will know that we are firmly rooted in Christ and are now built up in Him (Col. 2:7).

*We will know that we have been made complete in Christ (Col. 2:10).

*We will know we have been saved and set apart according to God's doing (2 Tim. 1:9, Titus 3:5).

*We will know we are partakers of a heavenly calling (Heb. 3:1).

*We will know we have a right to come boldly before the throne of God to find mercy and grace in time of need (Heb. 4:16).

*We will know we have been born again (1 Peter 1:23).

*We will know that we have been given exceedingly great and precious promises by God by which we are partakers of God's divine nature (2 Peter 1:4).

*We will know that we have been redeemed (Rev. 5:9).

Life works so much better when we have God in it. Just looking at this list shows the many benefits of knowing who we are in Him, who we belong to, and having a relationship with Him. We have great benefits when we know who we are in Him and go by His Leading at the end. We have great benefits when we know who we are in Him, and go by His leading.

Questions/Things to Think About

1. What traits do we gain by knowing who we are in the Lord?

_____

_____

_____

_____

_____

_____

2. What are some of the benefits of having a relationship with the Lord?

_____

_____

_____

_____

_____

_____

3. What are two things you can do to develop a relationship with God?

_____

_____

_____

_____

_____

_____

4. When we learn who we are in Him, what are some of the things we will know?

_____

_____

_____

_____

_____

_____

_____

5. When we know who we are in Him, what are two things we gain?

_____

_____

_____

_____

_____

_____

_____

6. What does Ephesians 1:2–6 explain?

_____

_____

_____

_____

_____

_____

7. How do you develop a relationship with the Lord?

_____

_____

_____

_____

_____

_____

8. What is the promise we gain in Philippians 4:6?

_____

_____

_____

_____

_____

_____

9. 2 Timothy 1:7 says we live from a place of?

_____

_____

_____

_____

_____

_____

_____

10. With all that you've learned so far, can you see
    how much life works better with our heavenly
    Father?

_____

_____

_____

_____

_____

_____

3: Get Planted in a Church/Ministry

One of the other things we have to do now that we are saved is to get planted in a church/ministry. The Word of God says, do not forsake the assembling together.

> *Not forsaking or neglecting to assemble together [as believers], as is the habit of some people, but admonishing (warning, urging, and encouraging) one another, and all the more faithfully as you see the day approaching.*

Hebrews 10:25 (AMP)

In order to get planted in a church, I encourage you to seek the Lord and ask Him to show you where you are to go for the ministry. The Lord will direct you and you will know, by your inner feeling, that this is where you are meant to go and fellowship.

An example of me asking the Lord where to attend church and fellowship was when I had moved to another area in my town. After moving, I asked the Lord where should I attend church? After asking the Lord where to attend, I kept seeing a church building in my spirit. I went to visit the church building and once I was there, I knew, from within, that that was where God wanted me to attend church and fellowship.

Another example, when I was in-between churches, was when my friend invited me to visit her church. Again, once I was there, I knew that that was where God wanted me to attend, worship, and fellowship.

There have been times where the Lord led me to leave a church. Sometimes the Lord has you in a church for a season. *Note: God always knows best.* So, even if I wanted to stay in the church, I had to follow God's leading. It can be challenging to leave a church, even though God is leading me, but I want to be in God's will so I will follow His leading.

It is important to follow the leading of the Lord to attend a church because not all churches are of God. In learning the things of God, I realized that some churches sound like God is in it, but it's really of Satan, portraying that it is of God. I experienced this. We have to be very careful where we attend church, which is why we have to seek the Lord, and ask Him where to attend church.

The Word of God says Satan acts as an angel of light:

> *And no wonder! For Satan himself transforms himself into an angel of light. Therefore it is no great thing if his ministers also transform themselves into ministers of righteousness...*

2 Corinthians 11:14–15

From my experiences, I know this to be true.

There are people that stay in churches for many years. If that is what the Lord leads you to, so be it. We have to make sure the Lord shows us where to go and that we are in His will as to where to attend His bethel, a holy place.

When we are planted in a church/ministry, we are taught the things of God, we get edified, we grow in the Lord, we develop our God-given gifts. When we are in church, we strengthen one another. The Bible says, "Iron sharpens iron" (Prov. 27:17).

> *New Living Translation note: Mental sharpness comes from being around good people. And a meeting of minds can help people see their ideas with new clarity, refine them, and shape them into*

brilliant insights. This requires partners who can challenge one another and stimulate thought—people who focus on the idea without involving their egos in the discussion, people who know how to attack the thought and not the thinker. Two friends who bring their ideas together can help each other become sharper.

I can attest to the iron sharpening iron because when my friends and I are talking, we will say something to one another we build up one another, and say, that was good and we will say, "Iron sharpens iron." We learn from one another in a positive way. I say in a positive way because we can learn from one another in negative ways. This is why it's so important to learn these steps once we are born again.

Being in a church helps us to learn more about God and not only learn, but fellowship with others, and serve others; thereby doing the work of the Lord.

We gain a lot by attending church. We get to share with others, and this is important as we learn from one another and the plus is, it helps us to not be an easy target of the enemy. Fellowshipping with others helps to provide us with protection and encouragement

For me, I love church. I always have, even when there was a time in my life that I strayed from it and wasn't attending church, church was always in me. Really, it was God in me.

Another reason it is important to be planted in a church/ministry is that we are to do the work of the ministry. We are all called to do the work of the Lord, we called are to serve. Also included is Ephesians 4:12, "*for the equipping of the saints for the work of ministry, for the edifying of the body of Christ.*"

Another aspect is that there is more regarding the church than just the building. It has many parts to it. The church building cannot run itself. The church/ministry needs people to help run it, it will need to be cleaned, there has to be helpers to lead the people, ushers to greet everyone, etc. All the functions in a church/ministry need to be filled in order for the church/ministry to run effectively and in proper order. Some functions are: the pastor, counseling, praise and worship leading, praying, musicians, etc. With these things properly in place, the church runs well.

All in all, the mission of the church is to:

- Be Christ's witnesses (Luke 24:45–49; Acts 1:7–8)

- Build up the body of Christ (Eph. 4:11–13)

- Do good to all people (Gal. 6:10; Titus 3:14)

- Exercise spiritual gifts (Rom. 12:6–8)

- Financially support God's work (1 Cor. 16:1–3)

- Help mankind in need (1 John 3:16–18)

- Love one other (Heb. 13:1–3, 16)

- Make disciples (Matt. 28:19–20)

- Offer hospitality to each other (1 Peter 4:9–11)

- Preach the Word (Mark 16:15–16, 1 Tim. 4:6,13)

- Take care of orphans and widows (1 Tim. 5:3–4,16; James 1:27)

- Take care of the sick (James 5:14–15)

When you look at this list, it shows the "whys" of why it is important to not forsake the gathering together and to attend church/ministry. We need one another to build up God's kingdom, to help one another, to learn to let the light of Christ shine through us so that others can be drawn to Him in order to be saved and live a successful life on earth.

Questions/Things to Think About

1. Why is it important to be planted in a church/
   ministry?

   _____

   _____

   _____

   _____

   _____

   _____

2. Should you go to any church? How will you
   know what church to attend? How do you de-
   termine where to go?

   _____

   _____

   _____

   _____

   _____

3. Why is it important to not just go to any church?

_____

_____

_____

_____

_____

_____

_____

4. What is meant by "iron sharpens iron"?

_____

_____

_____

_____

_____

_____

5. What happens to us when we go to church?

_____

_____

_____

_____

_____

_____

6. What are some of the things we are to do in church?

_____

_____

_____

_____

_____

_____

7. When we learn of God and let His light shine through us, what does that do?

_____

_____

_____

_____

_____

_____

_____

8. Name four things that are the mission of the church?

_____

_____

_____

_____

_____

_____

9. Ephesians 4:12 talks about what?

_____

_____

_____

_____

_____

_____

_____

10. What are two things needed to help the church run well?

_____

_____

_____

_____

_____

_____

4: The Devil (Our Enemy)

After being born again, we need to learn about the enemy of our soul. It's another must, and it's important even though all the things to do once saved are important.

We have an enemy that we are to learn and know about because he has a negative plan for our lives. Technically, this needs to be taught to children because they will grow up knowing of Satan's devices and will know to not fall into his wicked schemes.

We have to learn about our enemy, the devil, or Lucifer; these are some of the names of Satan.

We have to learn how the enemy of our soul operates in our lives and what he tries to do to us.

The devil is our enemy who hates us because we are God's creation, and he sets up schemes against us for us to fail, see John 10:10a

The Bible tells us what the devil does. This is why it is so important to meditate on the Word of God day and night (as is said in Joshua 1:8) in order to learn what we have, what we need to watch out for, how to conduct our lives, etc.

I have had many things happen to me in my life, and before knowing about our real enemy, Satan, it was the norm for me to fall into the traps he set and also to blame others. This is why I believe children should be taught this instead of learning this as an adult, like I did. If I had this knowledge from when I was a child, it would have saved and prevented a lot of hurt and misery for me. And I would have seen beforehand what the devil was trying to do. As a result of learning about how the enemy operates, I now recognize when the devil is trying to work in my life and also in the lives of others.

We have to recognize how the enemy operates in order to not be deceived. "Lest Satan should take advantage of us; for we are not ignorant of his devices." (2 Cor. 2:11). We have to recognize the enemy's devices in order to pray about it and not fall for it, and to be prepared in advance of the attacks.

One of the things that the devil does is goes around like a roaring lion seeking whom to devour. 1 Peter 5:8 (AMPC) says:

Be well balanced (temperate, sober of mind), be vigilant and cautious at all times; for that enemy of yours, the devil, roams around like a lion roaring [in fierce hunger], seeking someone to seize upon and devour.

With the devil going around seeking whom to devour, this shows that he watches us to see who doesn't know what they have in God and also, who is not saved, even the saved and then pounces on them and makes harsh attacks on their lives.

One of the attacks on my life happened at my birth. When I was born, words were said to me that charted my life on a negative path. The words were not meant but because they were said to me, they got in my spirit. The words were "What an ugly thing this is." Those words were from Satan who comes to steal, destroy, then kill (John 10:10a.)

The devil's schemes are not overnight. We can see something that looks good and go for it, then down the road, many years later, everything falls apart. For instance, David (a story from my book, *Are You in God's Will? Do You Know That You Have to Choose or Not?)* committed adultery for years before his wife got wind of it and the result of that was the family fell apart. All the devious plan of the enemy.

This is why it is extremely important to be saved and learn what we have in God, and to apply God's words to our lives because it helps us to live this life in a much better way and have positive results.

When I look back over my life, I can see when the enemy started something and then years later, that's when the damage showed up. For example, I was an emotional eater, and I know when the emotional eating started but I didn't know that that was what I was doing until years later, when so much damage was already done. Note: I talk about the food addiction story in my book *Food Addiction: The Struggle Has Been Real*.

Satan is the great deceiver (Rev. 12:9) who comes as an angel of light (2 Cor. 11:14) who will trick anyone who is not rooted and grounded in the Lord and His Word, which why I will continually say, it is extremely important to study, meditate, and apply the Word of God to your life. This way, Satan cannot trick or deceive you, especially when he comes as an angel of light. There have been times I fell for the trick of Satan, but when I realized this, I quickly changed and remember that weapons will form, but they won't prosper.

As is said in John 10:10, the thief, Satan, tries to take our life away from us whereas, our Lord and Savior gives life. The life our Lord gives is abundant and rich. With our heavenly Father, life is lived on a higher plane because of His overflowing love and guidance. We will always have a great life with the Lord.

Satan is the father of lies, John 8:44 (AMPC) says:

> *You are of your father, the devil, and it is your will to practice the lusts and gratify the desires [which are characteristic] of your father. He was a murderer from the beginning and does not stand in the truth, because there is no truth in him. When he speaks a falsehood, he speaks what is natural to him, for he is a liar [himself] and the father of lies and of all that is false.*

In order to know if we are hearing false words, we need to analyze them. We can ask God to confirm the words. Due to the subtlety of the devil, his lies can be seen as if there is truth to it. I've experienced this where I thought God was talking to me in a situation when it was actually the devil. It sounded so true, but it wasn't. To me, it's a thin line with regards to hearing the enemy because he knows the Word of God. Note that Satan was once in heaven, so it's extremely important to know how he operates to not be caught up in his subtle lies. The enemy's tactics are to divide and concur. An example of his tactics was Eve, see Genesis 3:1–6. The enemy was alone with her and twisted the words of God. *See the subtlety?* We have to be so alert to the devices of the enemy.

Even though we have to know the devil and how he works, we also have to know how to resist him, James 4:7 says: "Therefore submit to God. Resist the devil and he will flee from you." This is how we resist the devil, by subjecting to God, and how do we subject to God, through His Word. As we apply His Word to our lives, it will give us the strength to resist the devil.

The devil sets us up for a fall. I was talking with someone who was telling me the actions of a sibling. Because of learning how the enemy works, I let the person know that that is a set-up for a fall. When we study the Bible, we will learn how the devil operates and will know when he has set us up for destruction and can combat it with the knowledge from God's Word.

It is extremely, extremely important to learn about the wiles of the devil to not fall for the traps. He is always looking for ways to deceive us and take us out of the will of God. Being in the will of God helps us in a great and mighty way.

We have to note that Satan hates us because we are God's creation, we are children of God. It doesn't matter the age; from the youngest to the oldest, Satan hates us, so he always tries schemes to defeat us, to get us off course, and to discourage us, to distract us.

However, when we learn how Satan works, we will see the forming of things and know how to combat them and stop them in their tracks before damage is formed.

The bottom line to Satan is, he will try any scheme to try to get us off course. He is so subtle that we need God, and we need one another to not get caught up in his wicked schemes. One way is to use our God-given power and authority, and another way is being accountable to one another. As we share things with each other, we are able to catch the subtle schemes and stop them before things go completely wrong.

Just like being in the army, they learn the ways of the enemy in order to combat them, so make sure to learn the ways of our unseen enemy, it's imperative. Once we know how the enemy works, we will see when things are forming and not fall for them. However, as we are not perfect human beings, sometimes we can get caught up in the devil's schemes, but we will eventually recognize it and immediately make changes for it.

Even though we have an enemy, the Bible says that no weapon formed against us will prosper, see Isaiah 54:17.

Questions/Things to Think About

1. Are you aware that Satan has a plan for your life?

_____

_____

_____

_____

_____

2. How can you recognize the set-up of the enemy?

_____

_____

_____

_____

_____

_____

3. Are you understanding that we need to know how the devil operates?

_____

_____

_____

_____

_____

_____

4. How do we learn how the devil works?

_____

_____

_____

_____

_____

_____

_____

5. What does 2 Corinthians 2:11 say?

_____

_____

_____

_____

_____

_____

6. What is one of the things the enemy goes around and tries to do?

_____

_____

_____

_____

_____

_____

_____

7. What is one of the traits of the enemy (hint Rev. 12:9)

_____

_____

_____

_____

_____

_____

8. How do you resist the enemy?

_____

_____

_____

_____

_____

_____

9. Does the enemy have power over you?

_____

_____

_____

_____

_____

_____

_____

10. What can you do to have power over the enemy?

_____

_____

_____

_____

_____

5: Renew Your Mind (Unlearn and Relearn)

Another thing we need to do with salvation is to renew our minds by reading and studying the Bible.

The act of renewing your mind becomes the most important task a new believer has, and not doing so is a number one reason people backslide. It is important to renew our minds because, if we don't, our lives will not change. We'll remain doing the same things that are not beneficial to us, and it helps to prevent backsliding.

Think about it this way: the things you see and hear go into your memory. The things we read, watch on television, or listen to all affect us. We have to be careful of what we read and listen to because they shape our minds. If we watch negative things, our minds will become negative. When we renew our minds to God's perspective, we will have positive minds. That is why it is so critical to pay attention to what we watch and what we listen to. What is in your mind is what will ultimately manifest in your daily decisions and actions.

Note that the more you do something, see something, hear something, the more of your memory is taken up by those things. Think about it, when you hear a song that you've known for years but that you didn't hear for a long time, doesn't it come right back to your memory? The renewing of your mind needs to become one of the very first priorities in your new life with the Lord which is why it is a "to do" in this book.

For example, before my mind was renewed, I would say whatever came to my mind, but since renewing my mind, I now think about what I say before I speak it out of my mouth.

Why do we need to renew our minds? We are to renew our minds to think the way God thinks. This is another reason renewal of the mind is so important. When our minds are not renewed to think from God's perspective, sorry to say, we are thinking from the world's perspective and that is Satan.

Mind renewal is critical because our thinking controls our lives. How we think affects us. The way we feel, our desires, and our actions produce results in our lives.

Critical: crucial, extremely important because of being or happening at a time of special difficulty, trouble, or danger, when matters could quickly get either worse or better.

Produce: cause something. To cause something to happen or arise.

Actions: Doing something toward a goal. The process of doing something in order to achieve a purpose. Something done. Something that somebody or something does.

Before we are born again and renew our minds, as I mentioned, we think from the world's perspective and that is actually Satan's perspective. We have to renew our minds to not think from Satan's point of view.

Note: before we were born again, Satan was our father:

> *Ye are of your father the devil, and the lusts of your father ye will do. He was a murderer from the beginning, and abode not in the truth, because there is no truth in him. When he speaketh a lie, he speaketh of his own: for he is a liar, and the father of it.*

John 8:44 (KJV)

However, now that we are born again, God is now our heavenly Father.

We have to work on changing our minds from the world's way (Satan's way) of thinking and doing to God's way (our heavenly Father's) of thinking and doing. That is to look at things from God's perspective.

Another reason it is critical to renew our minds is that there won't be a life change. Without a mind change, our lives will remain the same, there will be no change.

> *Do not be conformed to this world (this age), [fashioned after and adapted to its external, superficial customs], but be transformed (changed) by the [entire] renewal of your mind [by its new ideals and its new attitude], so that you may prove [for yourselves] what is the good and acceptable and perfect will of God, even the thing which is good and acceptable and perfect [in His sight for you].*

Romans 12:2 (AMP)

Without a renewed mind, as Romans 12:2 says, our lives will remain the same as they've always been. In fact, it doesn't get better, no matter what we try. No matter how many times you study the Bible, no matter how many scriptures you read, no matter how much you go to church, no matter how much you pray and worship the Lord, if you mind isn't renewed, (have a mind change) the same problems, the same defeats will be had. We will keep going around the same mountain. An example of this was when I was in a relationship for years complaining about the same things without change because my mind wasn't renewed; this is going around the same mountain.

Jeremiah 48:11 is an illustration of no change without the renewal of the mind.

How do we renew our minds?

We renew our minds by the Word of God. As we study and meditate on His Words, we will think and act differently, thus the renewing of our minds.

The Bible says, the Word of God is not to depart from our mouths, meditating on it day and night (Josh. 1:8). As we meditate on the Word of God day and night, our minds are renewed to God's mind and way of thinking by applying His words to our lives.

"*And be constantly renewed in the spirit of your mind [having a fresh mental and spiritual attitude]*" (Eph. 4:23, AMPC). And how do we do that? By the Word of God.

Constantly means: continuously over a period of time; always.

Renewed means: having been resumed, re-established, or revived.

In life, we have to continually make decisions (all throughout the day), and we have to make sure we are thinking on good things to make the right decisions. I use Philippians 4:8 as a reference for this because it says to think on good things. For example, before my mind was renewed, I moved from one job to another. This eventually ended up being a bad move and I was laid off from the new job. If my mind was renewed back then, I'd have sought the Lord and done things differently.

Our Thoughts

We control our thoughts, yes, we sure do. Philippians 4:8, KJV, says to think on these things:

Finally, brethren, whatsoever things are true, whatsoever things are honest, whatsoever things are just, whatsoever things are pure, whatsoever things are lovely, whatsoever things are of good report; if there be any virtue, and if there be any praise, think on these things.

This shows that we control our thoughts.

A lot of things that come to mind are from different sources. They come from God, the devil, and ourselves, from what and who we listen to.

With our thoughts, they dictate our lives. We need to make sure we are thinking good and right thoughts so our lives will be victorious; thus the renewing of the mind.

There was a time in my life that I wasn't controlling my thoughts. I would say whatever came to my mind. In doing this, it would make circumstances worse because the words were harsh at times. With a renewed mind, I control my thoughts and control what I speak forth out of my mouth. The Word of God says to cast down wrong imaginations, see 2 Corinthians 10:4–6.

One day, I was talking with a co-worker who told me he couldn't sleep because he was thinking about all the work he had to do. I told him he could have changed his thoughts and went to sleep. His response was, "I can't change my thoughts." So many truths that we have to learn, unlearning what was learned and relearn. I am proof that we can change our thoughts as the Word of God says, to cast down wrong imaginations, thus the renewing of the mind.

Operate in the Fruit of the Spirit

One of the things with renewing the mind is, we are to operate from a different place than we are used to. We can do this by using Galatians 5:22–23, KJV, as our guide. It says, *"But the fruit of the Spirit is love, joy, peace, longsuffering, gentleness, goodness, faith, meekness, temperance..."*

This helps us to renew our minds with regards as to how we treat others. Let's take kindness from this scripture as an example. When someone is mean to us, the tendency is to be mean back to the person, but we are to love people from God's perspective, so we would treat them with kindness instead. When we react this way, our minds are renewed.

Bottom line is, you have to clean out the old thoughts and information in your mind and replace them with God-inspired information. Think like God thinks. Think from God's perspective.

Renewing your mind doesn't happen overnight. It is a process, a continual, daily process. So, make sure to keep at it.

Questions/Things to Think About

1. What is renewal of the mind?

   _____

   _____

   _____

   _____

   _____

   _____

2. Why is mind renewal important?

   _____

   _____

   _____

   _____

   _____

   _____

   _____

3. Why is what you read and listen to important?

_____

_____

_____

_____

_____

_____

_____

4. What scripture can you use to help with your thoughts?

_____

_____

_____

_____

_____

_____

5. Before we renew our minds, whose perspective are we thinking from?

_____

_____

_____

_____

_____

_____

6. What will happen if we don't have a mind change?

_____

_____

_____

_____

_____

_____

_____

7. Do you understand that you are in control of your mind?

_____

_____

_____

_____

_____

_____

_____

8. Will you make sure to work on renewing your mind?

_____

_____

_____

_____

_____

_____

9. How can you be sure you are renewing your mind?

_____

_____

_____

_____

_____

_____

10. What steps will you take?

_____

_____

_____

_____

_____

_____

6: Learn to Pray

What is prayer?

Prayer is talking and interacting with God, our Heavenly Father. The act of praying is a method of changing a situation for the better. Prayer is also petitioning God for our desires, see Jeremiah 29:12: *"Then you will call upon me and come and pray to me, and I will hear you."*

Prayer is one of the greatest gifts God has given to us. We get to talk with our heavenly Father anytime, 24/7, and it helps us to be closer to Him.

Why do we need to pray?

Praying is part of our duties as a born-again believer. As we pray, and pray continually, we will be changed into His image. There is also power in prayer.

There are different reasons for praying, praying for others, praying for healing, praying for yourself, praying for deliverance, and many more reasons to pray. We are to pray about and for all things in life, our spouses, our children (and/or grandchildren), our jobs, the government, *everything!*

In the Bible, there are many scriptures that talk about praying. I will mention a few here and you can research and study more on your own.

1 Thessalonians 5:17, KJV: *"Pray without ceasing."* Pray, pray, pray continually. To pray without ceasing is to never stop praying.

In fact, we are to live a life of prayer. I pray all day long, while washing the dishes, while I'm walking, while I'm working, and when I go to the store. I've learned to prayer no matter what I am doing.

1 Timothy 2:8, KJV: *"I will therefore that men pray everywhere…"* God works in our lives by our prayers. So, it is important to always be prayerful.

Psalms 55:17, KJV: *"Evening, and morning, and at noon, will I pray, and cry aloud: and he shall hear my voice."* This verse is showing us to pray morning, noon, and night, again, praying continually. The Lord hears us when we pray. I love for the Lord to hear me when I pray, how about you?

Matthew 26:41, KJV: *says, "Watch and pray, that ye enter not into temptation: the spirit indeed is willing, but the flesh is weak."* We will be tempted in life, and the way to help with the temptation is to pray. As this verse says, the spirit is willing but the flesh is weak. Continue to pray that we gain God's strength to be a defense against Satan's temptations.

Mark 11:24, AMPC: says to pray and believe that you will receive. *"For this reason, I am telling you, whatever you ask for in prayer, believe (trust and be confident) that it is granted to you, and you will [get it]."*

We have to believe for things before we see the results because things can be chaotic and not look like they will ever change. When we believe what we are praying for, it takes the focus off the circumstances at hand. For example, when I was experiencing issues on my job, it looked like things were not going to work in my favor, but as I prayed continually and believed for the right outcome, eventually everything turned around in my favor. In this way, it helps us to continue being in joy, peace, and happiness knowing that things will change. And as the saying goes, *"this too shall pass."*

Luke 11:1, KJV: *"And it came to pass, that, as he was praying in a certain place, when he ceased, one of his disciples said unto him, 'Lord, teach us to pray, as John also taught his disciples.'"* This scripture shows that we can ask the Lord to teach us to pray. There is no excuse to not pray. Pray the Word. Buy prayer books. Just pray…

James 5:13, KJV: "Is any among you afflicted? let him pray…" We are to pray for all those in our lives, including the sick. As we pray, we speak the right words and believe that healing will take place.

Prayer is so important that we get help in praying from the Spirit. Romans 8:26 says:

> *Likewise the Spirit also helpeth our infirmities: for we know not what we should pray for as we ought: but the Spirit itself maketh intercession for us with groanings which cannot be uttered.*

ॐ॰ॐ॰ॐ॰ॐ॰ॐ॰ॐ॰ॐ॰ॐ॰ॐ

I pray and talk with God every day, all throughout the day. Whatever issue comes up, I speak with the Lord about it. I even talk to God beforehand to help prevent things from happening. It is imperative that we speak with the Lord and listen for His guidance. This makes for a successful life.

You can use the scriptures to pray. Whatever the situation you are in, find the scriptures that pertain to it, and pray them (with believing that you receive) until you have breakthrough.

Examples of using scriptures to pray:

- If you are sick, stand on the promise in 1 Peter 5:8 and pray continually until you are healed.

- If you need favor, pray Psalm 5:12 (KJV), *"For thou, Lord, wilt bless the righteous; with favour wilt thou compass him as with a shield."* [Note: I pray Psalm 5:12 every day and thank God for His favor.]

- If you are feeling anxious, Philippians 4:6, *"Be careful for nothing; but in every thing by prayer and supplication with thanksgiving let your requests be made known unto God."*

- For your children (or grandchildren), "My children are taught of the Lord and great is their peace" (Isa. 54:13).

- If you are feeling fearful, pray 2 Timothy 1:7, *"For God hath not given us the spirit of fear; but of power, and of love, and of a sound mind."*

It is important to pray continually because the enemy is always on the prowl, see 1 Peter 5:8, looking for ways to defeat us.

A sample prayer is what is known as "The Lord's Prayer," Matthew 6:9–13 (KJV):

After this manner therefore pray ye: Our Father which art in heaven, Hallowed be thy name. Thy kingdom come, Thy will be done in earth, as it is in heaven. Give us this day our daily bread. And forgive us our debts, as we forgive our debtors. And lead us not into temptation, but deliver us from evil: For thine is the kingdom, and the power, and the glory, forever. Amen.

You can use prayer books, for instance, one of the prayer books I like is *The Power of a Praying Parent* by Stormie Omartian.

We are to pray for others, not just ourselves. When we see a need, pray. When someone is ill, pray. Pray for all things in life.

You can have a place to pray. A place that is dedicated for prayer. When you create a place to pray, you are choosing to make a specific space in your life dedicated to praying to our heavenly Father. Remember that a place to pray goes beyond a physical location, it is to be a way of life.

When you are new to praying, ask God to show you how to pray, and He will.

We can pray strategically. For instance, when a situation arises, you can find the scriptures that pertain to it and pray them until things come to pass. For example, if you have a financial problem, use the following scripture: "*Owe no one anything except to love one another.*" (Rom. 13:8).

It is important to pray continually because we have an adversary that is always trying to come against us. I talk more about the adversary in the chapter titled "The Devil."

Just pray, that's all.

Questions/Things to Think About

1. Why do we need to pray?

_____

_____

_____

_____

_____

_____

_____

2. Why do we need to pray continually?

_____

_____

_____

_____

_____

_____

3. If we are not praying to God, what will or will not happen?

_____

_____

_____

_____

_____

_____

_____

4. Analyze your life to see what you need to pray for:

_____

_____

_____

_____

_____

_____

5. Pray for others:

_____

_____

_____

_____

_____

_____

_____

6. Make a list of things to pray for:

_____

_____

_____

_____

_____

_____

_____

7. If you don't know what to pray, what can you do?

_____

_____

_____

_____

_____

_____

8. If you need favor in a situation, how do you pray for it?

_____

_____

_____

_____

_____

_____

9. Think about a situation you have going on now and find the scriptures that pertain to it, and pray them:

_____

_____

_____

_____

_____

_____

10. Create your own prayer journal. This helps you to keep track of your prayers and the answers.

_____

_____

_____

_____

_____

_____

7: Learn to Fast

We are now going to talk a bit about fasting, another thing to do when we are born again.

Fasting the biblical way, is refraining from food for a spiritual purpose. For example, Daniel fasted to cleanse his body and better focus on a spiritual connection to God, leaving behind the distractions.

Throughout the scriptures, people have fasted for many reasons. The main thing is, the Lord wants us to fast for the simple fact of what fasting does for us.

Fasting releases God's supernatural power. It is a tool we can use when there is opposition to God's will. Satan is the author of negative things that cause division, discouragement, defeat, depression, and doubt among us. When we fast, it's a blow to the enemy!

When we fast, from God's perspective, we eliminate food from our diets for a specific number of days. When we do this, our spirits become uncluttered by the things in our lives and in the world, and in turn, it makes us more sensitive to the things of God. For instance, when I fast, I will get more clarity on situations.

When we fast on a regular basis, we will see that fasting is a secret source of power that I didn't realize until I began fasting. When I started fasting:

1. I saw a huge difference in my prayers being answered

2. I saw that I was much more sensitive to God

3. I saw that I gained more clarity

Just these three things alone show us how important it is to fast.

Isaiah 58 talks about the right and wrong way to fast; and that fasting looses the chains of injustice, to set the captives free. I encourage you to read it. Here is a portion:

Isaiah 58:5 (AMP) says,

Is such a fast as yours what I have chosen, a day for a man to humble himself with sorrow in his soul? [Is true fasting merely mechanical?] Is it only to bow down his head like a bulrush and to spread sackcloth and ashes under him [to indicate a condition of heart that he does not have]? Will you call this a fast and an acceptable day to the Lord?

We are to fast for the right reasons. It's easy to fast by not eating but is it the right reason? There have been times where I ended up not eating for hours, and it crossed my mind that I could call it a fast. But this won't be the right reason, so I don't call it a fast.

The Bible talks about not fasting as the hypocrites did.

> *Also when you pray, you must not be like the hypocrites, for they love to pray standing in the synagogues and on the corners of the streets, that they may be seen by people. Truly I tell you, they have their reward in full already.*

Matthew 6:5 (AMPC)

We are to fast as unto the Lord. Matthew 6:17 recommends that we don't publicize our fast. The only time I will publicize it is if I'm offered a meal or something to eat. This is when I'll say I'm fasting, or just say "No, thank you."

Another thing fasting does is it humbles us. Fasting is a sign of humility. It keeps us modest and have a low view of our own importance that helps to keep the focus on our Lord. As we focus on the Lord, we make choices that lead to a life of success and victory.

With fasting, you are emptying yourself before God. In this way, you are allowing the Spirit of God to then use you to do His good work—like healing, teaching, etc. Walking in your purpose in a greater way.

There are other aspects as to why fasting is important. The Bible says there are things that go out but by prayer and fasting, see Matthew 17:21. We can have situations in our lives that we have prayed about, sometimes for years, that when we fast, it breaks it. *There is power in fasting.*

Prayer and fasting:

But when you pray, go into your [most] private room, and, closing the door, pray to your Father, Who is in secret; and your Father, Who sees in secret, will reward you *in the open.* And when you pray, do not heap up phrases (multiply words, repeating the same ones over and over) as the Gentiles do, for they think they will be heard for their much speaking. Do not be like them, for your Father knows what you need before you ask Him. Pray, therefore, like this: Our Father Who is in heaven, hallowed (kept holy) be Your name. Your kingdom come, Your will be done on earth as it is in heaven. Give us this day our daily bread. And forgive us our debts, as we also have forgiven (left, remitted, and let go of the debts, and have given up resentment against) our debtors. And lead (bring) us not into temptation, but deliver us from the evil one. *For Yours is the kingdom and the power and the glory forever. Amen.* For if you forgive people their trespasses [their reckless and willful sins, leaving them, letting them go, and giving up resentment], your heavenly Father will also forgive you. But if you do not forgive others their trespasses [their reckless and willful sins, leaving them, letting them go, and giving up resentment], neither will your Father forgive you your trespasses. And whenever you are fasting, do not look gloomy *and* sour *and* dreary like the hypocrites, for they put on a dismal countenance, that their fasting may be apparent to *and* seen by men. Truly I say to you, they have their reward in full already. But when you fast, perfume your head and wash your face, So that your fasting may not be noticed by men but by your Father, Who sees in secret; and your Father, who sees in secret, will reward you *in the open.*

Matthew 6:6–18 (AMPC)

Listed here are some fasts that were done, from the Bible, and it also shows us what fasting can do:

- Fasting was an expected discipline in the Old and New Testament eras. For example, Moses fasted at least two recorded forty-day periods. Jesus fasted forty days and reminded His followers to fast…"when you fast," not if you fast.

- Fasting and prayer can restore the loss of the "first love" for your Lord and result in a more intimate relationship with our heavenly Father.

- Fasting is a biblical way to truly humble yourself in the sight of God (Ps. 35:13; Ezra 8:21). King David said, "I humble myself through fasting."

- Fasting enables the Holy Spirit to reveal your true spiritual condition, resulting in brokenness, repentance, and a transformed life.

- The Holy Spirit will quicken the Word of our heavenly Father in your heart and His truth will become more meaningful to you!

- Fasting can transform your prayer life into a richer and more personal experience.

- Fasting can result in a dynamic personal revival in your own life—and make you a channel of revival to others.

- Fasting and prayer are the only disciplines that fulfill the requirements of 2 Chronicles 7:14:

If my people, who are called by my name, will humble themselves and pray and seek my face and turn from their wicked ways, then will I hear from heaven and will forgive their sin and will heal their land.

Anyone can fast, it's not limited at all. See Jonah 3:5, AMPC:

So the people of Nineveh believed in God and proclaimed a fast and put on sackcloth [in penitent mourning], from the greatest of them even to the least of them.

This verse shows that anyone can fast, so there is no excuse for not fasting.

You can schedule your fasts. For instance, fast every Wednesday, every beginning of the month, etc. Jentezen Franklin conducts a twenty-one-day fast at the beginning of every year that I have joined. *Fasting is powerful.*

When you fast, you will find yourself being humbled as I did. You will discover more time to pray and seek God's face. And as He leads you to recognize and repent of unconfessed sin, you will experience special favor from God.

There are many verses on fasting. I encourage you to study fasting on your own to learn more about it.

Questions/Things to Think About

1. What is fasting?

---

2. Why is it important to fast?

---

3. What is the reason fasting is a secret source of power?

_____

_____

_____

_____

_____

_____

_____

4. Read Isaiah 58 and think about what it says to fast in the right way.

_____

_____

_____

_____

_____

_____

5. With fasting, you are emptying yourself before God. What does it do for you?

_____

_____

_____

_____

_____

_____

6. What is an aspect to why fasting is important?

_____

_____

_____

_____

_____

_____

_____

7. What does Matthew 6:6–18 say about prayer and fasting?

_____

_____

_____

_____

_____

_____

8. What are two types of fasting that were done in the Bible?

_____

_____

_____

_____

_____

_____

_____

9. What is fasting the biblical way?

_____

_____

_____

_____

_____

_____

10. When I started fasting, what was one thing that happened as a result?

_____

_____

_____

_____

_____

_____

_____

8: Get Wisdom and Understanding

Why is "get wisdom and understanding" part of the must dos when we are born again, you ask?

One of the things I'm known for is my wisdom and understanding which is why I know this is another thing that we need to do when we are born again, spiritually. Also, Proverbs 3:13 talks about being blessed when you find wisdom and get understanding.

"That people may know skillful and godly wisdom and instruction, discern and comprehend the word of understanding and insight," Prov. 1:2, AMPC. This shows that we will have great success when we use God's wisdom.

Also see Colossians 1:9: "…that ye might be filled with the knowledge of His will in all wisdom and spiritual understanding," and Colossians 1:10: "…increasing in the knowledge of God."

The book of Proverbs is full of wisdom and understanding (I suggest you study the book of Proverbs often.) I read a book of Proverbs every day each month, and it is suggested that we read Proverbs each month for a year. For example, starting January 1, read Proverbs 1; January 2, read Proverbs 2; January 3, read Proverbs 3, so on and so forth, and our lives will change.

In order to have the right wisdom and understanding, we have to get God's wisdom (that is putting God first) and understanding to live life well on earth. Otherwise, life is harder and will be full of hard knocks. My own experiences with getting God's wisdom and His understanding has made my life much easier as I seek God first. This is another thing that doesn't happen overnight, but as we keep seeking God first, it gets easier and easier, and actually becomes the norm. We are actually unlearning and relearning.

Since I've studied the Bible, read many spiritual books and magazines, listened to many sermons, watched a lot of godly programs, I have gained a lot of knowledge and understanding that has helped me a great deal in my life in a positive way.

Wisdom is the quality of having experience, knowledge, and good judgment; the quality of being wise. Wisdom helps us to discern what's right from what's wrong. It gives us the capability to make right choices.

Having knowledge is power, and with wisdom, we use power in the right way.

Wisdom is practical. As we apply wisdom to our situations, we overcome them positively.

Wisdom is divine. God's wisdom is beyond common sense, and those without it don't always understand.

Wisdom is being God-like. As we ask and use wisdom given from God, we are living from His direction.

Below are some things to do to gain wisdom because we have to learn it. It doesn't just come to us; we have to do something to get it. (Note: we are born empty and it's what we fill ourselves with that determines if we have wisdom.)

Steps to Gain Wisdom

1. Ask for wisdom from our heavenly Father (James 1:5). When we ask for wisdom, God will give it to us. We can ask for God's wisdom to help us in life's circumstances, especially difficult ones.

2. Ask faithfully. Hebrews 11:6 talks about it being impossible to please God without faith. Having faith is believing for what we don't see.

When we ask faithfully, we are already believing for what we've asked for.

3. Be a God-loving person. When you have love God, you follow His teachings and do what they say.

4. Be humble. With humility, it's admitting you don't know; thus, we ask the Lord.

5. Be prudent. Prudence is related to wisdom because you will act in accordance with the right reason, thus being wise.

6. Be peaceful and considerate. When we use wisdom, we will be peaceful and considerate.

7. Read the Holy Scriptures, know the words of God, and apply them to your life. This is how we gain wisdom, the wisdom that helps us to make right choices.

8. Know our Lord better, as chapter 2 talks about. As I always say, "we have so much in God, we just have to learn it."

Life has obstacles that come our way all the time, in fact, daily. But having and using wisdom helps us to make right choices that lead to victory.

Before gaining the wisdom, I have now, I made choices based on my own wisdom, and many of those choices didn't lead to a victorious life. One of the decisions I made resulted in having debt. If I had used wisdom, I wouldn't have gotten into debt.

In using wisdom, we will stop and think before making decisions.

When we are wise, we think before we do things, and we count the cost before doing anything.

An example of using wisdom was when someone contacted me regarding issues they were having on their job. I gave suggestions on how to handle the situation using the wisdom I've gained over the years. Later that day, the person contacted me to let me know that what I had advised had worked. I am thankful, because without using wisdom, I don't know what I would have advised, and it may not have ended up as victorious.

Make sure to apply the right wisdom, that is God's wisdom, to your circumstances and you will live a victorious life .

Questions/Things to Think About

1. What is the definition of wisdom?

_____

_____

_____

_____

_____

_____

2. What does Proverbs 1:2 talk about?

_____

_____

_____

_____

_____

_____

3. Will you read a chapter of Proverbs per day as is suggested in this chapter?

_____

_____

_____

_____

_____

4. How do we get the right wisdom?

_____

_____

_____

_____

_____

_____

5. When we don't have the right wisdom, what happens to us?

_____

_____

_____

_____

_____

_____

6. What is the promise found in Proverbs 3:13?

_____

_____

_____

_____

_____

_____

7. Why is it important to use wisdom in our circumstances?

_____

_____

_____

_____

_____

_____

_____

8. How do we gain wisdom?

_____

_____

_____

_____

_____

_____

9. What happens when we don't use wisdom in our circumstances?

_____

_____

_____

_____

_____

_____

10. Think about your circumstances that are happening now and apply wisdom to them.

_____

_____

_____

_____

_____

_____

9: Watch Your Words

One of the most important things we have to do when we are born again, spiritually, is to learn to watch our *words* because we get what we say; our words dictate our lives. I cannot *emphasize* this enough. Our own words, that come out of our own mouths, sets us up for failure or success.

"Death and life are in the power of the tongue, and those who love it will eat its fruit" (Prov. 18:21).

As we renew our minds, as is spoken about in chapter 5, this helps us to learn to watch our words. To be careful of what we speak. What we need to do is to speak positive words only.

I understood the importance of our words a little bit because many years ago, I would say I wanted to be sick because I would get time off of work, I wanted to be home with my children. I didn't mean those words, but upon saying them, I eventually got sick. I got so sick that I had to have emergency surgery. With this happening to me, I knew to stop saying those words. *With this story, can you see how the words that I said got me to be sick, and I stayed home? I got what I was saying.*

However, even with me getting sick based on the words that I was saying, I still didn't have the full revelation of how important my words were and I continued to speak negative words that affected my life in a negative way.

About twelve years ago, I read the book called *How to Avoid Tragedy and Live a Better Life*. As I was reading this book, words I would say were coming back to my memory. My life had become the words I had said back then. *What a revelation!*

Since reading the Charles Capps book, I have changed the way I say things. I often change the words around in my mind before I speak them out. Unlearning *what* I have learned.

We have to think and speak differently to have the life we want (again renewing the mind), which is really the life God wants us to have. Our words are a vital key of what we must do since being born again.

Upon learning that the words we say will dictate our lives, my words have changed a lot. For instance,

I used to say, "Stop doing that because you could get hurt." Instead, I turned it around and now say, "Because you could get hurt, stop doing that." How I used to say it before, the last words were "get hurt." The last words being said and heard are what counts.

Another thing I would say is "poor thing." By saying this, forces went to work to make sure I was poor and whoever else says it, stays poor.

The phrase "poor thing" has been said in my family for generations, and I hear people tell them all the time. Its meaning is not wishing anyone to be poor, but meaning you feel sorry for them, an endearing term. What a subtle way the enemy has us twisting our words to pronounce wrong things on our lives and other's lives.

There are many examples of wrong words being said that has formed negativity in people's lives, instead of positivity. And the good thing is, it's all learned behavior that makes it easy for us to make changes.

I had to unlearn a lot of words I would say, and I'm still unlearning.

Let's look at what Proverbs 18:21 says, *"Death and life are in the power of the tongue, and those who love it will eat its fruit."* Meaning, what we say is what we get.

If we say we are poor, we are going to stay poor. If you don't believe me, check your life and check the words you say about your life. I'm living proof that what we say we get.

Now, let's look at what Proverbs 16:24 says, *"Pleasant words are like a honeycomb, sweetness to the soul and health to the bones,"* meaning, saying positive things, is better for you.

For me, I continue to make sure I'm saying the right words. I continually analyze my words before I speak them out of my mouth. Always remember that our own words frame our world, and it's the same for all of us, no one is exempt.

What we say out of our mouths comes to pass. We have to be very careful what we speak out of our mouths. We even have to be careful what we think. What we think, becomes spoken words.

Another verse I live by is 2 Corinthians 10:5, "casting down arguments and every high thing that exalts itself against the knowledge of God, bringing every thought into captivity to the obedience of Christ."

This scripture helps me to say the right things. If I'm thinking something wrong or if I'm about to say something that will make my life negative instead of positive, I've practiced remembering this scripture so that I change to a positive thought whenever a negative one arises. I advise you to adapt this too. *It works!* There will always be negative thoughts, but we can make sure to change them by following this simple guideline. (Note: I also have this scripture posted on my wall as a reminder.)

Many of us are not taught the importance of what we say affects our lives; well speaking for myself, I wasn't. The importance of our words needs to be taught at an early age so that children grow up saying the right words, saying positive words that will lead them to grow up and live a great born again life.

Before I learned the importance of words, I would say anything that came to mind. This is what made my life so negative. As I mentioned, when I read the book titled *How to Avoid Tragedy and Live a Better Life* by Charles Capps, this is when I learned, on a deep level, the extreme importance of what I say, the extreme importance of my words. I will always remember, as I was reading the book, the things that came back to my remembrance of what I would say that framed my world to have so much negativity in it. My words had made my life hell and I didn't know it was my own words that did it at the time.

When I received this revelation, I had told others about the importance of our words. Some have laughed at me and mocked me, telling me that it's just words, but I kept going on. Some have gotten it and are now careful with their words. One of my prayers is for God to open their eyes to the truth about the extreme importance of our words.

Examples of Words Said:

Someone's child was about to touch something, and the parent said, "Don't touch that," but the child still touched it. My antennas went off and my response was, the last thing the child heard was "touch that," so that is why the child still touched it. A light bulb went off to the parent saying, "That's true."

Another parent would say "My child doesn't listen." My response to that was, "Your child won't listen because you keep saying he won't listen. Change your words to 'my child listens,' and that's what you will get, your child will start listening to you."

This other person says to her brother, "You fool" and guess what, he is a fool.

A parent tells her son, "You are no good." Guess how the son is, yes, you're getting it, he is no good.

A husband would say to his wife, "You are once, twice, three times a lady" and guess what, she gained so much weight that she got to two times a lady and was on her way to three times a lady.

This lady I know would say to her son, "Don't follow your brother," because the brother was on a destructive path. You know the outcome, you guessed it, yup, he followed his brother. The last words he would hear were "follow your brother," and that's just what he did, followed his brother.

I've seen many instances where the negative words made an impact on people's lives in a negative way that led to destructive lives, instead of victorious.

I'm sure you are understanding the importance of our words. *What we say, is what we get!*

See Genesis 1 where God spoke, and the world was formed. Everything God spoke came to pass. His words framed the world.

The power of the tongue is real, see Proverbs 18:21. Study it for yourself and take heed to making sure that you are saying words that bring success and victory to your life as our words are a very important aspect regarding being born again.

What I say is *"speak the Word of God."* This way you are sure to say the right words, and His words don't return void, see Isaiah 55:11.

To reiterate, our words are extremely, extremely, important. I can't say it enough. Be very careful what you confess out of your mouth, it will come to pass. We've given Satan words to work with for too long already that have made a lot of our lives destructive. It's time to give God our words to work with to bring success and victory to our lives. Praise God!

Another one of my sayings is, "We're either giving Satan words to work with or we're giving God words to work with." We have to make sure we are giving God words to work with.

Note: we also have to be careful of the words other people say to us. This topic is for another time.

Now go and speak right words, life-giving words.

Questions/Things to Think About

1. Why is it important to watch our words?

2. What does Proverbs 18:21 mean to you?

3. What does renewing our minds help us to do?

_____

_____

_____

_____

_____

_____

4. What type of words do we need to speak?

_____

_____

_____

_____

_____

_____

5. What is the name of the book that gave the author the full revelation of our words?

_____

_____

_____

_____

_____

_____

_____

6. What does the author do in her mind before she speaks words?

_____

_____

_____

_____

_____

_____

7. What do wrong words said do to our lives?

_____

_____

_____

_____

_____

_____

_____

8. Why is Philippians 4:8 important to use?

_____

_____

_____

_____

_____

_____

_____

9. Share one story from the example words said:

_____

_____

_____

_____

_____

_____

_____

10. Who else do we have to be careful of regarding words?

_____

_____

_____

_____

_____

_____

10: Operate in Your Gifts

Why is "operate in your gifts" a must do now that we are saved? In 1 Peter 4:10, we're called to use our gifts to serve others as faithful stewards of God's grace in its various forms (NIV). Also, the Bible talks about some spiritual gifts in 1 Corinthians 12:8–10.

God has put a gift or talent in every person that the world will make room for. Proverbs 18:16 (NKJV) is a powerful statement that reveals this: *"A man's gift makes room for him."*

I believe we are all on this earth for a purpose. We all have our own unique gifts to help make the world a better place. Also, as we are born again, we are God's ambassadors on earth. With that being said, when we are born again, we are to seek our gift (if we don't already know what it is) and operate in our gift(s).

It is important to operate in our gifts so much so that 2 Timothy 1:6 says to stir up the gift.

Here is a list of gifts listed in the Bible:

1. Administration

2. Being an apostle

3. Discernment

4. Evangelism

5. Exhortation

6. Faith

7. Giving

8. Healing

9. Helps

10. Hospitality

11. Knowledge

12. Leadership

13. Mercy

14. Prophecy

15. Serving

16. Speaking in tongues

17. Teaching (sometimes known as shepherding)

18. Wisdom

Administration is the process or activity of running a business, organization, etc. In this case, the ability to help steer the church, or a ministry, toward the successful completion of God-given goals, with skills in planning, organization, and supervision.

An apostle is one who is sent; a person sent to new places with the gospel, to help spread the Word of God. An apostle can also provide leadership to other churches or ministries and offer advice on spiritual matters.

Discernment is a decision-making tool in which an individual makes a discovery that leads to future action. Discernment from God's perspective guides the individual to help them arrive at the best decision. Discernment is the wisdom to recognize truth from untruth by correctly evaluating whether a behavior or teaching is from God or another ungodly source in order to make the right decision.

Evangelism is the act of preaching the gospel to communicate the message of the gospel, especially to those need to believe.

Exhortation is defined as the act or process of making a strong urging or appeal. It's the capacity to offer encouragement, comfort, and support to help someone to be all that God wants them to be; reminding mankind of what we have in God.

Now faith is the assurance of things hoped for, the conviction of things not seen (Heb. 11:1, ESV). People with this faith have such great confidence in the power and promises of God that they stand strong in their belief, no matter what happens, or comes up.

Giving is the sense to give. Those who have this gift are willing to share resources that they have with delight, and without the need to see them returned. They are okay with giving and not receiving in return.

Healing is through divine intervention as in response to prayer or because of faith. A method employing prayer or faith in the hope of receiving such healing. A capability used by God to restore others, be that physically, emotionally, mentally, or spiritually.

Helps is to aid; to assist; to lend strength or means towards effecting a purpose; to assist; to lend strength or *means* towards effecting a purpose; as, as, to help a man in his work; to help another in. Someone with this gift is able to support or assist members of the body of the church so that they may be free to minister to others.

Hospitality is treating friends and strangers alike. It is welcoming one another into our homes and lives. Hospitality is a spiritual duty, as we are to take care of others from God's perspective. Hospitality is a natural ability to make people, even strangers, feel welcome in one's own home or church as a means to disciple or serve them.

Knowledge is facts, information, and skills acquired by a person through experience or education, the theoretical or practical understanding of a subject. This is the gift of someone who actively pursues knowledge of the Bible, the right knowledge.

Leadership is the action of leading a group of people or an organization. A church leader is a person who is able to stand before a church, to teach and direct the body with care and attention, and to motivate them toward achieving the church's goals, and the individual's purpose.

Mercy is compassion or forgiveness shown toward someone whom it is within one's power to punish or harm. This is a trait of a person with great sensitivity for those who are suffering. It manifests itself in offering compassion and encouragement, and in a love for giving help to someone in need.

Prophecy is the inspired declaration of divine will and purpose. The ability to speak the message of God to others. This usually involves foresight or visions of what is to come.

Serving, from a biblical perspective, is the purpose of service is so God can reach others through our hands. A talent for identifying tasks needed for the body of Christ and using available resources to get the job done. Also, we are God's handiwork, created for good works, see Ephesians 2:10.

Speaking in tongues is the supernatural ability to speak in another language (one that has not been learned). It is speech directly addressed to God, but also as something that can potentially be interpreted into human language.

Teaching is ideas or principles taught by an authority. Teaching is the skill to teach from the Bible and communicate it effectively for the understanding, edifying, and spiritual growth of others.

Wisdom is the quality of having experience, knowledge, and good judgment; the quality of being wise. Wisdom is the gift of being able to sort through facts and data to discover what needs to be done for the church.

If you are not operating in your gift(s) and are not sure what your gift(s) is, pray and seek the Lord.

One of the benefits of operating in our gift(s) is that we will feel fulfilled and experience more joy. I can attest to this, as one of my gifts is to teach victorious living.

And the other thing with us all operating in our gifts, things will work well; thus, making the world a better place.

There are questions on the next page that will help you in determining your gift(s), purpose, and passion. Make sure to operate in your gift(s). I believe we are all here for a purpose and we need to operate in them to fulfill our callings on earth. Also, as was said at the beginning of this chapter, in 1 Peter 4:10 (NIV), we're called to use our gifts to serve others as faithful stewards of God's grace in its various forms.

Questions/Things to Think About

1. What is your why?

_____

_____

_____

_____

_____

_____

2. What makes your heart sing?

_____

_____

_____

_____

_____

_____

3. What do you love to talk about?

_____

_____

_____

_____

_____

_____

4. What do you hate to stop doing at night?

_____

_____

_____

_____

_____

_____

5. What makes you cry, what makes you angry?

_____

_____

_____

_____

_____

_____

_____

6. Pay attention to what stirs your heart. Examine that as this is a clue to your gift(s), passions, and purpose.

_____

_____

_____

_____

_____

_____

7. Pay attention to your desires.

_____

_____

_____

_____

_____

_____

8. What comes easy for you?

_____

_____

_____

_____

_____

_____

9. What do you love to do?

_____

_____

_____

_____

_____

_____

_____

10. Who do you love to help, children, teens, adults?

_____

_____

_____

_____

_____

_____

_____

The ten basic things to do after salvation are:

1. Study the Word of God (the Bible) and apply it to your life

2. Learn who we are in our heavenly Father and have a relationship with Him

3. Get planted in a church/ministry

4. The devil (our enemy)

5. Renew your mind (unlearn and relearn)

6. Learn to pray

7. Learn to fast

8. Get wisdom and understanding

9. Watch your words

10. Operate In your gifts

When I learned these ten basic things to do after being born again spiritually, it was a game changer. My life began to transform from being so broken, mediocre, and stuck, and it continues to get better and better as I am continually learning and growing in the things of God. I hunger and thirst after Him and He fills me (Matt. 5:6).

We can live our best lives now, we can have joy, peace, and happiness all the time regardless of the circumstances. We just have to learn of the Lord and believe that we can. …with God, all things are possible (Matt. 19:26, Mark 10:27).

I hope this book is a blessing to you and that the things of God are taken seriously because we do have an enemy that tries to steal from us, destroy us, and kill us (John 10:10). However, in turn, we are His ambassadors on earth. We are here to make the world a better place from God's perspective, especially as we operate in our gifts.

I hope that you take heed to what we have to do now that you are saved. Being saved keeps you from going to hell when we pass on from earth, but we do have things to do while we are here. Once we apply these ten basic things, it will make our lives easier to handle. We'll make wise choices; we'll know how to handle life's affairs, handle what comes out way, we'll help others in a positive way, we'll count the cost, etc.

Note that as we're born again (spiritually) and begin to learn the things of God, it is a process and happens slowly over time as we continue to apply the Word of God to our lives.

With applying these ten basic things to our lives, we will begin to experience life more abundantly as promised in John 10:10b, and this is just the beginning. We will continue to grow in the Lord, gain more knowledge, wisdom, and understanding, we will be more like Him; and that is His desire.

Talk with me!

How did my book *Born Again, Now What? Ten Basic Things to Do After Salvation* help you? I'd love to hear from you with your reactions and thoughts.

Please comment at noreennhenry@gmail.com

"From a life of defeat to a life of victory"

Noreen N. Henry

Appendix One

Recommended Books

How to Avoid Tragedy and Live a Better Life by Charles Capps. This is the book that I received the full revelation of our words.

Victorious Living: Guide to a Happier Life, written by me. I wrote this book to help you with living victoriously.

Are You in God's Will? Do You Know That You Have to Choose? Also written by me to explain the difference between being in the Lord's will, and the consequences of not being in His will.

For the Already Saved

We give thanks that you are already saved, and your name is written in the Lamb's book of life, hallelujah! You will *not* be eternally separated from God.

Are you living the blessed life of health, wisdom, peace, and wealth? Are you doing the work of the ministry? If not, contact me via email at victoriousliving-ministries7@gmail.com, or in writing 1803 Nereid Avenue, #143, Bronx, NY 10466, and I'll show you how.

I pray that the saved are in God's will and plan for their lives. I pray that the saved know the power and authority that they have in the name of Jesus, that they operate in the gifts of the spirit as is said in the Word of God (1 Cor. 12 explains the use of the spiritual gifts), and having signs that follow them as is said in Mark 16:17–18:

And these signs will follow those who believe: In My name they will cast out demons; they will speak with new tongues; they will take up serpents; and if they drink anything deadly, it will by no means hurt them; they will lay hands on the sick, and they will recover."

The Bible says in Luke 10:2, "The harvest truly *is* great, but the laborers *are* few; therefore, pray the

Lord of the harvest to send out laborers into His harvest." In essence, this verse is saying that the world is full of people that need to be saved and that there are only a few saved that are laboring for the harvest.

The saved are to dedicate their skills to God's kingdom, be equipped with His power, and have a clear vision of what He wants us to do. We are to ask God for more workers. Also, we are not to just sit back and watch others work, we are to look for ways to help with the harvest.

Contact me for more information on what the saved are to be doing and how the saved are to be living the blessed life.

Glory to God!

About the Author

Noreen N. Henry is a Victorious Living Strategist, who is focused on living victoriously, living her best life now, and creating victorious habits for the life of your dreams. She is known for her knowledge, wisdom, and understanding along with instant results. One of her passions is transforming women's lives from defeat, stuck, mediocre, broken to victory. She is a powerful coach, international speaker, trainer, author, and health educator. She is an 8x #1 international best-seller, who published 21 books.

Noreen experienced many adversities that led to her learning tools to be victorious. As a result, Noreen founded Victorious Living Culture, a "Victorious Living 'Culture' movement," where her products and services help countless individuals turn their situations into victory and into their God-given life's purpose.

Noreen's native residence is London, England, and she migrated to the States in her late teens. She came from humble beginnings in a small town in East London and has progressed so much so that she was graced to be on a billboard on Broadway, in Times Square, New York City. She never dreamed she would be on a billboard, let alone in the heart of NYC.

Noreen obtained an AAS degree, and various certificates and diplomas. Noreen is an avid reader who continues to educate herself. She is currently enrolled in International School of Ministry's Bachelor's degree program. Noreen completed the Cornell's Women's Entrepreneur program and AmplifyHER Voice Speaker & Mentorship Certification Program. She continues to take courses to craft her talents.

Noreen is an ordained minister and is a certified Biblical Counselor. She is a member of the American Association of Christian Counselors, 4 Corners Alliance, John Maxwell Team Member, Toastmasters International, and Promote-Her. Noreen is also certified in: Administrative Assistant, Cake Baking and Decorator, Biblical Counseling, and GSC. She has acquired "Another Seat at The Table: Inclusion and Diversity Compliance License."

Noreen has been featured on Gratitude Girls, Authors in Business, National Black Book Festival, Visions of Greatness Entrepreneur Spotlight, Conversations with Lady Linda, Kingdom Purpose Talk, Courageous Woman Magazine, SNAPD Downtown Toronto, AmplifyHer Magazine, Divine Purpose Magazine, and various other media outlets. Some of Noreen's work has been seen on CBS, ABC, FOX, NBC, The CW. She created the "Unleash Your Greatest Potential, Living Your Best Life NOW!" Annual Event, and now has a TV talk show called "Victorious Living with Noreen" because "Stuck Is NOT Your Story."

Noreen is passionate about victorious living and cares a great deal about mankind. She is making the world a better place one person at a time. The song "People Help the People" was dedicated to Noreen by one of her nieces.

Noreen is the mother of three children, and four grandchildren, and resides in New York City. Reach Noreen on www.NoreenNHenry.com or at Victorious Living Culture's academy www.StartYourVictoriousLife.com

Noreen N. Henry is a "Victorious Living Strategist" who is mandated by the Most High to teach you how to live victoriously everyday of your life, and to teach you how to go through your trials and tribulations until you overcome them to victory while staying in a state of joy, peace, and happiness.

Noreen is full of wisdom. It was said that "people should sit at her feet and draw from her knowledge and wisdom."

Don't miss out on drawing from Noreen's experiences, knowledge, and wisdom, plus instant results.

She offers coaching programs and has many more programs in the works.

Contact Noreen to be coached or mentored at victoriouslivingculture@gmail.com or 1803 Nereid Avenue, MB 143, Bronx, NY 10466.

Noreen thanks you in advance for your trust in her to coach or mentor you.

"Victorious Living Culture's

Products and Services"

Website: www.NoreenNHenry.com

****

"One-on-One Coaching"

Click here for a strategy session

www.calendly.com/noreennhenry

****

Victorious Living Culture's Academy

www.StartYourVictoriousLife.com

****

7–Week Signature Program

This program comes with great bonuses that are gifts to you.

Email: victoriouslivingculture@gmail.com   for more info

****

Click here for your FREE gift of my victorious living worksheet: http://eepurl.com/cVhsVH

Note: You'll have to add you first name and email address to receive this.

COMING SOON!

Facebook.com/VictoriousLivingWithNoreenT-VTalkShow

Youtube:
https://tinyurl.com/YouTube-Noreen-N-Henry

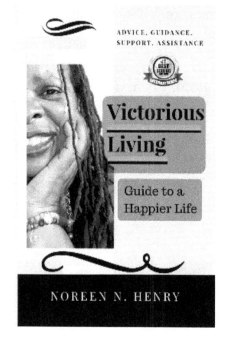

As seen on:

For your own autographed copy, click here:

https://www.noreennhenry.com/product-page/victorious-living-guide-to-a-happier-life

eBook: http://amzn.to/2rVFIhR

Paperback:https://www.amazon.com/dp/1492760080

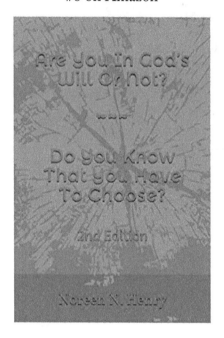

This book has a companion workbook.

The workbook makes you think deeply about your choices and helps you to understand that the things of God are important. It helps you to make wise choices that lead to a better life for all.

For your own autographed copy, click here:

https://www.noreennhenry.com/product-page/are-you-in-god-s-will-or-not

ebook: https://www.amazon.com/dp/B06XGVY3G3

Paperback:https://www.amazon.com/Are-You-Gods-Will-Not/dp/1520800703

In honor and memory of my mum:

"Top 100 on Amazon"

Ebook: https://www.amazon.com/dp/B07GFL6JQJ-US

Paperback: https://www.amazon.com/dp/1720110417

Autographed copies click here:

https://www.noreennhenry.com/product-page/legacy-journal

"Top 100 on Amazon"

ebook: https://www.amazon.com/dp/B07L7J1LS3

Paperback: https://www.amazon.com/dp/1794172696

Autographed copies click here: https://tinyurl.com/yaealdj4

"#1 in Hot New Releases"

MULTIPLE #1 INTERNATIONAL BEST SELLER

A LEGACY BOOK

INTERESTING FACTS JOURNAL

NOREEN N. HENRY

ebook: www.amazon.com/dp/B07TSL777D

Paperback: www.amazon.com/Legacy-Book-Interesting-Facts-Journal/dp/1708517510

For autographed copies:

https://tinyurl.com/ALegacyBook

T-Shirts and Canvas Bags

Upcoming:

DAILY SCRIPTURES HELP TO KEEP MY FOCUS WHERE IT
SHOULD BE. IT'S A GREAT WAY TO START MY DAY.
-DEE THOMAS

Muliple #1 Int'l Bestselling Author

On pre-sale now

Click here to order your autographed copy

https://tinyurl.com/Daily-Scripture-Journal

Stay Connected:

Facebook:

https://www.facebook.com/noreen.n.henry

Linkedin:

https://www.linkedin.com/in/noreen-n-henry-72056913

Instagram:

www.instagram.com/victoriousnoreen

Twitter:

www.twitter.com/victorious7812

Look out for more books and products from

Victorious Living Culture in the near future.

Some are:

Healing

Your Family and Your Business

Scripture Journals

and much more to come.

Noreen thanks you in advance for your trust in her to coach, mentor, teach, and train you for your victorious living journey.

Note: when Noreen helps someone, it's fulfilling to her. She enjoys seeing people's lives change to positive, moving from brokenness, mediocrity, or being stuck, and that they stay in joy, peace, and happiness. Even though we go through trials and tribulations, we can still live a victorious life by gaining the right knowledge and using wisdom rightly. When we understand the good, we can have as we apply the right knowledge and wisdom, it will life changing, and your life will be unrecognizable. God favor your life, and God favor you.

Author's Note

∞

I pray that this book helps you

greatly in your born-again journey,

and will continue to bless you.

God bless your life, and God bless you

abundantly as you continue on His path

to live victoriously every day now that

you are born again.

"Always live spiritually minded!"